CooL STAMPS

Creating Fun *and* Fascinating Collections!

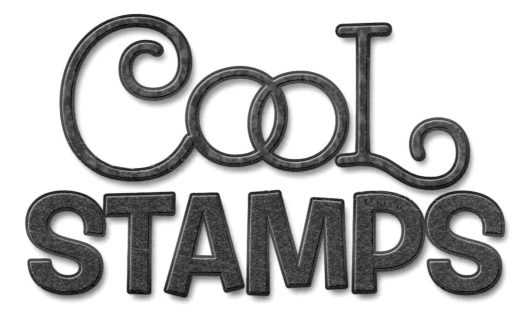

Pam Price

ABDO
Publishing Company

Visit us at
www.abdopublishing.com

Printed in the United States.

Design and Production: Mighty Media, Inc.
Cover Photo: Anders Hanson
Interior Photos: Anders Hanson; Shutterstock; Easter Seals (p. 10) appear with permission of and are copyright by Easter Seals Inc.; dog stamp (p. 15) © PhotoStamps.com, used with permission; The *2002 Scott Standard Postage Stamp Catalogue* appears with permission of Amos Hobby Publications; *The Unitrade Specialized Catalog of Canadian Stamps*, 2006 edition, used with permission from Unitrade Associates, Toronto, Canada; self-printed album pages appear with permission of StampAlbums.com; Supersafe Prefolded Stamp Hinges. Used with permission from Vidiforms Company.

Special thanks to Fred Schiffman, Crossroads Stamp Shop, for sharing both his knowledge and his stamp collection.

Library of Congress Cataloging-in-Publication Data

Price, Pamela S.
   Cool stamps / Pam Price.
      p. cm. -- (Cool collections)
   Includes index.
   ISBN-13: 978-1-59679-774-1
   ISBN-10: 1-59679-774-6
   1. Stamp collecting--Juvenile literature. I. Title. II. Series: Cool collections (Edina, Minn.)

HE6213.P75 2007
769.56--dc22

2006011997

Contents

WHEN THE UNITED STATES WAS FIRST ESTABLISHED, THERE WERE NO STAMPS. And, people didn't put letters in envelopes. The cost of sending a letter was partly based on the number of sheets of paper. So, people simply folded up the letter, sealed it with wax, and wrote the address on it.

The person who received the letter paid for the delivery. And it was expensive! It cost about 6 cents to send a letter 30 miles or less and up to 25 cents to send a letter 450 or more miles.

This led to some **unscrupulous** behavior. Sometimes, the sender would write a note in code on the outside of the letter. The recipient would read the coded message as the letter was being handed to him. Then he could refuse the letter and not have to pay for its delivery.

In the United States, this practice came to an end in 1847. That's when the first official postage stamps were introduced. The 5-cent stamp bore the image of Benjamin Franklin (left). George Washington was on the 10-cent stamp.

It cost 5 cents per half ounce to mail a letter under 300 miles. It cost 10 cents per half ounce to mail a letter more than 300 miles. As the roads became better and travel was easier, postage rates came down. By July 1, 1885, you could mail a one-ounce letter anywhere in the United States for two cents.

The United States was not the first country to issue postage stamps, though. That honor went to Great Britain in 1840. That first stamp, called the Penny Black, featured a portrait of Queen Victoria on a black background.

Only a year later, an advertisement appeared in the newspaper requesting stamps. The buyer wanted to use them to paper a bedroom wall. Thus was stamp collecting born!

By the 1860s, stamp dealers had set up businesses. The first stamp catalogs and albums became available. In 1886, the American Philatelic Society was formed. Today it is the largest nonprofit stamp-collecting society in the world.

Famous stamp collectors have included U.S. president Franklin D. Roosevelt (above) and King George V of England. Many kings in many countries have collected stamps, which is perhaps why stamp collecting is called the hobby of kings.

But stamp collecting isn't only for kings. It's a great hobby for anyone. You will enjoy stamp collecting if you like organizing things. You will enjoy stamp collecting if you like to learn fun facts about people, places, and things all over the world. So let's get started!

**WHEN YOU'RE FIRST GETTING STARTED,
PICK UP A FEW STAMP CATALOGS.** Go to a stamp shop or even
a stamp show. Just browse until you get a feel for what the options are and what
captures your interest. Don't get hung up on building a valuable collection, though.
Most collections are barely worth the face value of the stamps.

Mint or Used?

A mint stamp has never been used. It is in the same condition as when the post office
issued it. Some people collect mint stamps because they are worth more than similar
used stamps.

Used stamps have been stuck on an envelope and postmarked. People who collect used
stamps like that the stamps bear the marks of their travel around the world. Stamps
that have never been mailed but are not in perfect condition are called unused stamps.

Single-Country Collections

Most stamp collectors start out with
worldwide collections. Eventually
they choose one country's stamps
to collect. Often this is the country
they live in or the country their
ancestors came from.

Topical Collections

In a topical collection, all the stamps relate to one topic. They may come from different years and countries, but they all have the same topic in common. Use a stamp catalog to research stamps that might fit your topic.

Popular Topics

States

Animals

Famous people

Buildings

Historic events

Transportation

Stamp Types

Post offices around the world issue several different types of stamps. These are some of the most common types.

DEFINITIVE

Definitive stamps are the workhorse stamps. They are usually first class stamps or **makeup** stamps. They are small in size and are often printed in a single color. Over time, billions of copies of a definitive stamp will be printed and sold by the post office.

COMMEMORATIVE

Commemorative stamps are printed to honor people, historic events, statehood anniversaries, organizations, and causes. Commemorative stamps are larger than definitive stamps. They can be very colorful. Commemorative stamps are printed in smaller quantities than definitive stamps and are not usually reprinted.

SPECIAL

Special stamps are similar to commemorative stamps, but the post office is more likely to reprint them when the supply runs out.

SEMIPOSTALS

Semipostal stamps are fundraising stamps. They cost more than other stamps. The extra money you pay for these stamps goes to the charity featured on the stamp.

OTHER POSTAGE STAMPS

There are special stamps for some mail services. These include airmail, postage due, special delivery, parcel post, and registered mail.

CINDERELLA STAMPS

Some stamps don't have anything to do with postage. These stamps are called Cinderellas. Cinderellas are also sometimes called back-of-the-book stamps. That's because listings for Cinderella stamps appear after the postage stamp listings in catalogs. They are in the back of the book!

Duck stamps are required on some hunting licenses. Proceeds from the stamps help support conservation efforts. These stamps are quite beautiful. Each year a contest is held to select the artist who will design the next federal duck stamp. You can buy duck stamps at the post office, but you can't use them to mail letters!

Revenue stamps show that tax on a product has been paid. The United States began taxing many documents and goods to help pay for the Civil War. Items that were taxed included licenses and permits, playing cards, matches, medicines, and photographs.

A Cinderella Story

In 1934, the National Society for Crippled Children began distributing seals to raise money. The seals they issued each Easter became so popular that the organization was renamed in 1967. Can you guess the new name? Well, Easter Seals, of course! Easter Seals still issues new seals each spring.

Stamp Shapes and Formats

Some people collect stamps that have special shapes, such as circles, triangles, and pentagons. Some countries issue **die-cut** stamps in shapes such as fruit or flowers.

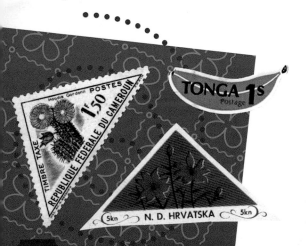

Errors

Sometimes mistakes pay—for the collectors, that is! Some of the most sought-after stamps are those with printing errors. Errors can be hard to come by. It's U.S. Postal Service policy to destroy errors.

Stamps printed with an upside-down image are called inverts. There are only 11 known inverts among all the U.S. stamps. The inverted Jenny is one of the more well-known. Printed in 1918, the Jenny was the first U.S. airmail stamp. The airplane on the stamp, a Curtiss JN-4 biplane, was somehow printed upside down.

Postal workers discovered and destroyed eight sheets of the misprinted stamps. But before the error was discovered, one sheet of 100 stamps was sold. A block of four of these stamps sold for $2.7 million in 2005.

Postmarks

Postmarks give you a clue to the history of the stamp, especially where and when it was mailed. If you collect postmarks, look for those that are clearly printed and centered over the stamp.

In the language of stamp collectors, an envelope is called a cover. Of particular interest to some collectors are first day covers (FDCs). A first day cover consists of the envelope, the stamp, and a postmark dated on the first day the stamp was released. Never remove a stamp from an FDC. The value is in the combination of envelope, stamp, and postmark.

Today the post office announces the date and city where a new stamp will be released. You can learn when new stamps will be issued and how to get FDCs at the post office.

Most FDCs issued since the 1920s include a cachet. A cachet is a special illustration printed on the left side of the cover.

Color My World

This stamp looks perfectly fine to most people. So consider this. In the United States, certain stamps are supposed to be certain colors. When this stamp was issued, one-cent stamps were green. Two-cent stamps were red. And, five-cent stamps were blue. Now do you see the error?

Where to Get Stamps

IT'S EASY TO FIND USED STAMPS TO START A COLLECTION. You can get them from letters that come to your house. You can ask neighbors and friends to save the stamps they get in the mail. You can even ask local businesses to save their stamps for you. Ask them to leave the stamps on the envelopes so you can soak off the stamps yourself (see page 26).

If you want to get stamps from other countries, get a pen pal. The American Philatelic Society (APS) and other stamp-collecting groups have services to match stamp collectors around the world. Before joining a pen pal group, talk to a parent or other adult who can help you make sure it is safe to join.

You can also buy used stamps. Stamp shops and stamp dealers often sell bags of U.S. or foreign stamps for just a few dollars. You won't find rare or valuable stamps in these grab bags, but you will find plenty of cool stamps to start your collection.

As your collection grows, you will identify specific stamps you need to complete an album page or a set of stamps. That's when you should create a wants list. Write down the name of the stamp, its country of origin, its Scott number (see page 16), the grade you want, and the price you are willing to pay.

Take your wants list whenever you go to shows, swaps, and shops. It will help you stay focused and keep you from overbuying or overpaying.

STAMP SHOWS

Stamp shows are great places to get stamps and learn more about stamp collecting. You can learn when and where stamp shows will be held by talking to local stamp clubs and stamp shops.

Dealers set up booths at shows to sell stamps. Most of them will have rare and expensive stamps for sale. This is a great chance to see these stamps in person and learn more about them. Most dealers will also have less-expensive stamps available, either in bags or still on the covers.

If you see something you would like to buy, it's okay to ask for a small discount. Just be polite and ask quietly. You never want to put a dealer on the spot in front of other customers. The way these questions are usually phrased is, "Is this your best price on this stamp?" or "Are you offering any discounts today?"

Here's one thing that people who attend shows of all types know. If you are looking for something special, go early. If you are looking for bargains, go late.

New stamps

The post office is the place to buy new stamps. Try to go when it's not busy. Then you can spend some time looking at all the stamps available. You can also learn about new stamps that will be issued later. And the clerk will be able to tell you how to get first day covers of the new issues.

ART OF THE AMERICAN INDIAN

If you live in or near a big city, ask your local post office where the nearest Philatelic Center is located. These centers are located in the main post office. They are designed to help stamp collectors. They offer a wider range of stamps and stamp-related materials than smaller post office branches can. You can also learn about new issues and FDCs online at the official U.S. Postal Service Web site.

What's a Philatelist?

You are a philatelist! A philatelist is someone who collects and studies postage stamps and related materials. Philately is the act of collecting and studying postage stamps. If something is described as philatelic, that means it is related to stamp collecting.

Make Your Own!

Did you know that you can get personal stamps? You upload a photograph, choose a border, and pay for the stamps online. The stamps are sent to you in the mail. The stamps are approved by the U.S. Postal Service, so you can use them to mail things. Check it out at http://photo.stamps.com.

ONLINE

Many dealers and shop owners now sell stamps online too. Some have online stores with fixed prices. Others sell through auction sites such as eBay. When you begin collecting, stick to buying in shops and at shows. Don't buy online until you know more about stamps and collecting. And for safety's sake, always have an adult help you when you do buy online.

When buying online, look at the photos carefully and read the descriptions. Read what to do if you get the stamp and it is in worse condition than described. Decide ahead of time what you are willing to pay. Most auction sites provide a way to check the sellers' reviews and ratings. Look for sellers with high ratings and good feedback.

Researching Your Stamps

ONCE YOU BUY A BUNCH OF STAMPS, YOU HAVE TO IDENTIFY THEM SO YOU CAN ORGANIZE THEM IN AN ALBUM. Sometimes this can take some real detective work. Some stamps look alike, but you may find they are very different once you learn more about them. Here are some of the tools philatelists use to identify their stamps.

Stamp Catalogs

Catalogs list stamps by country and date of issue. They include pictures, which makes it much quicker to narrow down which stamp you have. You can buy stamp catalogs or get them at the library.

Scott Standard Postage Stamp Catalogue is a six-volume set that lists all postage stamps issued worldwide. It is updated every year. Each stamp in the catalog is assigned a number. These numbers have become a standard for stamp collectors. Many collectors and dealers use the Scott numbers to identify their stamps.

The Postal Service Guide to U.S. Stamps contains color photographs of more than 4,000 U.S. stamps issued since 1847. It also includes duck stamps, specialty postage stamps, and postal stationery. It uses the Scott catalog numbers. It is a good reference for U.S. stamps.

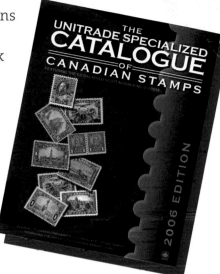

The Unitrade Specialized Catalogue of Canadian Stamps lists Canadian stamps. It has color pictures and current values. It uses the Scott numbers.

There are also many specialty catalogs. Some catalogs list stamp errors and oddities. Others are pocket-size price guides. There is even a guide to help identify stamps that have no writing on them.

What's in a Name?

Remember that countries can and do change names. For example, Siam became Thailand, went back to Siam, and is now Thailand again. Whew! So if you can't find a country listed in a catalog, see if it's listed under a former name.

Ready, Set, Sort!

IF YOU BUY A BIG GRAB BAG OF FOREIGN STAMPS, FIRST SORT THEM BY COUNTRY. Then use catalogs to identify what you have. Store stamps you can't identify in **glassine** envelopes or stock pages until you have time to identify them.

Stock pages are handy for sorting. They have pockets that run across the page. You just slip the stamps into the pockets and leave them there until you're ready to mount the stamps.

You can buy special trays for sorting a lot of stamps. You can also use plastic boxes with small compartments. These are available at craft stores and hardware stores.

Temporary storage devices make it easier to stop sorting and put away your work. But they have another advantage too. They help keep your stamps from blowing around if someone walks by or your cat jumps up!

What's It Worth?

THE MAIN REASON TO COLLECT ANYTHING IS BECAUSE YOU ENJOY IT.
Making a profit on a collection is rare. But it's still fun to know the value of what you collect. In addition, it's important to know the value of stamps you want to buy.

Several factors determine the value of stamps. One is the law of supply and demand. If a stamp is rare and a lot of people want it, its price will be high. If a stamp is common and there isn't a lot of demand for it, its price will be low.

Also consider the value of the stamp to you personally. Imagine you need only one stamp to complete a collection. You might be willing to pay a bit more to get that stamp. You might also be willing to pay extra for a stamp that completes a set.

The value of a stamp may vary widely, depending on its condition and grade. Condition is the combination of factors that affect how a stamp looks today.

Ask the Expert

People who buy and sell very rare, expensive stamps often get them "expertized." The expert examines the stamp and certifies its authenticity and condition. Experts help buyers avoid stamps that are counterfeit, regummed, or reperforated. It costs $20 or more to have a stamp expertized.

Stamp Grades

There are standards for grading stamps, but opinion enters into grading. Any two people might see slight differences in a stamp's condition and assign it different grades. These grades refer to a stamp's centering, margin width, **perforations**, and cancellation.

Average (AVG)   **Fine (F)**   **Very fine (VF)**

Superb (S). The stamp image is perfectly centered with equal margins on all sides.

Extremely fine (EF). The stamp image is almost perfectly centered and the margins are almost perfectly balanced.

Very fine (VF). The stamp image is slightly off center on one side, but well clear of the edge. Cancels on used stamps are light and clear.

Fine-very fine (F-VF). The stamp image is off center toward one side or slightly off on two sides. The cancel on used stamps does not **detract** from the design.

Fine (F). The stamp image is noticeably off center on two sides. Stamp perforations may barely clear the design on one side. With very old stamps, the perforations slightly cut into the design. Used stamps may have somewhat heavy cancels.

Average (AVG). The image is very poorly centered, and the perforations cut into the image. Cancels on used stamps are heavy and detract from the image.

Gum Condition

Dealers use other abbreviations to state the condition of the stamp. Most of these relate to the gum. These are some of the common abbreviations. There are plenty of other abbreviations, though. If you run across an abbreviation you don't know, ask the dealer what it means.

Never hinged (NH). A hinge has never been attached to the stamp, and its gum is original and near perfect.

Lightly hinged (LH). A hinge was attached to the stamp, but the gum is barely disturbed as a result.

Heavily hinged (HH). The hinge was so firmly attached that part of it remains or a great deal of gum was removed along with the hinge.

Original gum (OG). The stamp has all of the gum that was applied when the stamp was made.

Disturbed gum (DG). Part of the gum has been removed, either from hinging or through a **mishap** such as becoming stuck to the album page.

Regummed (RG). Believe it or not, there are services to apply new gum to stamps. Regumming may make a stamp look better, but it decreases the value.

No gum (NG). All of the original gum is gone, which reduces the value of the stamp considerably. Note that some stamps were originally issued without gum, which does not reduce their value. These are referred to as issued without gum or ungummed instead of no gum.

STAMP COLLECTING DOES NOT REQUIRE A HUGE INVESTMENT IN TOOLS AND MATERIALS. These are the basic supplies you will need to get started.

Albums

You can buy stamp albums for specific countries. These have preprinted pages that indicate which stamps to collect and where they go. As new stamps are issued each year, the album manufacturers print new pages to hold the new stamps. The packages of new pages are called supplements.

Specialty stamp albums range in price. Although some are not too expensive, others can cost hundreds of dollars.

A less-expensive alternative is a simple three-ring binder and less-expensive pages. One option is **quadrille**-ruled pages. Instead of boxes, these have a grid to help you align the stamps. These are nice pages for topical collections because you can arrange the stamps any way you want.

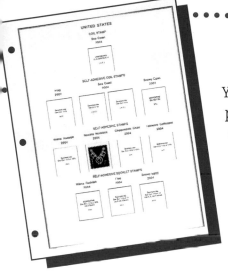

You can print your own pages with inexpensive software. These pages usually don't have pictures of the stamps on them. But, many do have boxes and catalog numbers to show which stamps go where.

Keep two things in mind if you print your own pages. Use heavy paper so the pages aren't floppy and you can't see through them. Even more important, use acid-free, archival-quality paper. The acids in ordinary paper seep out over time and can damage your stamps.

Photo albums and scrap books with archival-quality paper pages also make good stamp albums. Don't use photo albums with sticky pages because they can damage your stamps.

No matter how many or what kinds of albums you get, choose expandable albums. Then you can add and rearrange pages.

Album Tips

- Always store albums standing upright. The weight of stacked albums may make stamps stick to pages.

- Don't add too many pages to an album. When there are too many pages, the pages will curve, and so will your stamps.

- Put stamps on only one side of the pages. When you put stamps on both sides, the stamps on facing pages can catch on each other and tear.

Hinges

Stamp hinges were invented in 1889. Before then, collectors pasted stamps to wallpaper or glued them into books. This was not very good for the stamps!

Hinges are small, thin, folded strips of paper or plastic. They have adhesive on one side. Do not use tape or glue instead of hinges or mounts. Tape and glue decrease the value of stamps and make it hard to remove the stamps from the album.

Hinges are good for mounting used stamps. Don't use them on mint or unused stamps because removing the stamp from the hinge damages the stamp's adhesive. Hinges are cheaper than mounts. They don't add much bulk to an album.

Mounts

Mounts are clear, plastic sleeves that are open on the sides. You can buy them sized to fit most standard stamp sizes. You can also buy them in strips and cut them to size.

Mounts are more expensive than hinges, but they allow you to remove a stamp from the album without damaging the stamp. Mounts help protect stamps from dust and moisture. Mounts are thicker than hinges, so they do add bulk to the album.

Stock Cards

Stock cards are the size of index cards. They are useful for transporting stamps to and from shops and shows.

Tongs

Tongs look like long, thin tweezers. Unlike tweezers, they have a smooth gripping surface for grasping the stamp. Cosmetic tweezers have a sharp edge that will damage stamps. Always use tongs to handle stamps. Even clean hands have oil on the skin that can damage stamps.

Magnifying Glass

A magnifying glass helps you closely examine a stamp's details and condition. Choose a magnifying glass with a glass lens. A plastic lens can distort the image. A magnifier with 5- to 10-times magnification is all you need. Choose one with a case to protect the lens from dust and scratches.

Glassine Envelopes

Glassine envelopes are used for temporary storage of stamps. They are available in many sizes.

Handling Your Stamps

MANY OF THE STAMPS YOU COLLECT WILL STILL BE ATTACHED TO THEIR COVERS. The way to get them off is to soak them. Do not tear or peel the stamps off the envelopes. Even if you are very careful, you will likely remove some of the paper the stamp is printed on. This seriously reduces the quality and value of the stamp.

Soaking Lick-and-stick Stamps

First cut off the corner of the envelope. Place it in a bowl of lukewarm water with the stamp facing up. Do not use hot water because it can fade the stamps.

You can place a few stamps in the bowl at a time. However, soak brightly colored stamps separately. If the ink runs, it may ruin the other stamps in the bowl. Change the water in the bowl after soaking a few batches of stamps.

After a few minutes, the stamps should float free of the paper. Grasp each stamp gently with your tongs and place it on a paper towel. When the paper towel is full, put another paper towel on top. Set a book on top of the paper towels to keep the stamps from curling as they dry. Let the stamps dry overnight.

Look Before You Cut!

Look carefully at the entire cover, especially old covers, before deciding to remove the stamp. Sometimes the cover with the stamp still attached is worth more than the stamp alone. Likewise, never remove a stamp from a postcard. The postcard is usually more valuable than the stamp.

Self-adhesive Stamps

In theory, soaking self-stick stamps is the same as soaking lick-and-stick stamps. However, you may find it takes longer for the adhesive to release from the stamp.

Collecting mint self-stick stamps is a bit more complex. Because the adhesive is fairly new, no one knows for certain how it will affect the stamp over time. For example, the earliest self-stick stamps yellowed. The Postal Service has changed the adhesive, but we still don't know how those stamps will hold up over the decades.

People who are concerned about the adhesive damaging the stamp sometimes put the stamp on a piece of paper and soak it off. However, collectors of mint stamps place a great value on intact adhesive, so this may devalue the stamp, even though it's never been used.

Others choose to leave the stamp on its backing and mount it that way. Many stamps now have information about the stamp's subject printed on the backing. Mounting the stamp with its backing intact preserves this information.

Another option is to save entire sheets of stamps. Sometimes the entire sheet has many copies of the same stamp. This is called a plate block. Other sheets have several different stamps on the same sheet. These are called se-tenant sheets.

If the stamp you're mounting is in a sheet of stamps, remove the stamps around the one you want. Then neatly trim the backing around your stamp. Be very careful not to cut the stamp, and stay clear of the perforations!

You can save the stamps you removed to mail letters. Or, you can put them on paper and soak them off. This is a good idea because then your collection will have one copy of the stamp with its original backing and another with the adhesive removed.

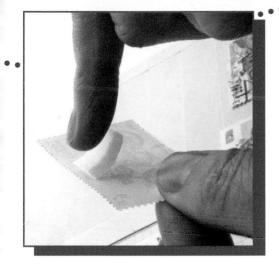

Hinges

To use a hinge, first moisten the short flap. You can lick either the hinge or your pinky to do this. Position the damp hinge one-third of the way down the back of the stamp. Then moisten the longer flap of the hinge and set the stamp on the page.

Be very careful not to wet the hinge too much. Excess moisture can squeeze out when you put the stamp in the album. This will wet the stamp's adhesive and may make it stick to the album page.

Mounts

You can buy mounts to fit most U.S. stamps. However, you'll have to buy mounts in long strips and cut them to length for other stamps. Always measure, then cut. It's tempting to put the stamp in the mount so you can easily cut the mount to the exact size. But, it's far too easy to also cut the stamp when you do it this way.

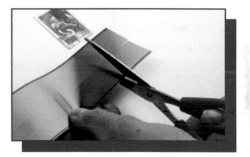

Carefully moisten the adhesive on the back of the mount and press it in place on the album page. After the adhesive dries, slip the stamp inside the mount. When you lick the mount, some moisture can seep inside the slit on the back of the mount. That's why it's important to wait a while before sliding the stamp into the mount.

When using mounts, take the page out of the binder so it lies flat while you work. Wait until all the mounts are set up before putting the page back in the album.

AS WITH ANY HOBBY, YOUR INTEREST IN STAMP COLLECTING WILL FADE AT TIMES. If you find you aren't interested in collecting, this may be a sign that you should collect different stamps for a while. Find a new topic and see if that sparks your interest again.

You may also find that you simply don't have time to work on your collection. Or you may get interested in other things, such as sports, a club, or a new hobby. That's okay. This happens to all collectors. Some people who start hobbies when they are young find they don't have time for them again until they are finished with school.

If you don't have time for or interest in collecting, just stash your collection and supplies somewhere that is cool, dry, and dark. Someday you will take it out again. You may decide to sell it at that point. Or, you might find that you want to start collecting again. That's how lifelong hobbies are born!

detract – to reduce the value or importance of something.

die-cut – a shape made by cutting paper with a die. A die is a steel cutter made to cut paper into a particular shape.

glassine – a thin, dense paper that is resistant to air and grease.

makeup – a stamp with a low price, such as two or three cents, that is used when postal rates are raised. It makes up the difference between the cost of an existing first-class stamp and the new postage rate.

mishap – an unfortunate accident.

perforation – a series of holes between stamps that allow you to easily separate them.

quadrille – marked with squares.

unscrupulous – without principles or honor.

Web Sites

To learn more about stamp collecting, visit ABDO Publishing on the World Wide Web at **www.abdopublishing.com**. Web sites about stamp collecting are featured on our Book Links page. These links are routinely monitored and updated to provide the most current information available.

Index